D0713060

COMMUNITY HELPERS

Reporters

by Kieran Downs

BELLWETHER MEDIA • MINNEAPOLIS, MN

Blastoff! Readers are carefully developed by literacy experts to build reading stamina and move students toward fluency by combining standards-based content with developmentally appropriate text.

Level 1 provides the most support through repetition of high-frequency words, light text, predictable sentence patterns, and strong visual support.

Level 2 offers early readers a bit more challenge through varied sentences, increased text load, and text-supportive special features.

Level 3 advances early-fluent readers toward fluency through increased text load, less reliance on photos, advancing concepts, longer sentences, and more complex special features.

★ **Blastoff! Universe**

Reading Level

Grade **K**

Grades **1–3**

Grade **4**

This edition first published in 2021 by Bellwether Media, Inc.

No part of this publication may be reproduced in whole or in part without written permission of the publisher. For information regarding permission, write to Bellwether Media, Inc., Attention: Permissions Department, 6012 Blue Circle Drive, Minnetonka, MN 55343.

Library of Congress Cataloging-in-Publication Data

Names: Downs, Kieran, author.
Title: Reporters / by Kieran Downs.
Description: Minneapolis, MN : Bellwether Media, Inc., 2021. | Series: Blastoff! Readers : community helpers | Includes bibliographical references and index. | Audience: Ages: 5-8 | Audience: Grades: K-1 | Summary: "Developed by literacy experts for students in kindergarten through grade three, this book introduces reporters to young readers through leveled text and related photos"– Provided by publisher.
Identifiers: LCCN 2019054238 (print) | LCCN 2019054239 (ebook) | ISBN 9781644871959 (library binding) | ISBN 9781681038193 (paperback) | ISBN 9781618919533 (ebook)
Subjects: LCSH: Reporters and reporting–Juvenile literature. | Journalism–Juvenile literature.
Classification: LCC PN4781 .D69 2021 (print) | LCC PN4781 (ebook) | DDC 070.4/3–dc23
LC record available at https://lccn.loc.gov/2019054238
LC ebook record available at https://lccn.loc.gov/2019054239

Editor: Betsy Rathburn   Designer: Laura Sowers

Printed in the United States of America, North Mankato, MN.

Table of Contents

Breaking News!

The team won the game! A reporter covers the story.

She **interviews** a fan. The story will be on the news!

What Are Reporters?

Reporters record things that happen. They **research** what they find.

Reporters work for **news outlets**. They often travel to cover stories.

What Do Reporters Do?

Reporters find events to report on. They tell people what happened.

Reporter Gear

microphone   camera   pencil   notebook

13

Reporters look for **sources**. These back up their reports.

Reporters share
what they learned.
Stories are in

newspapers or on TV.
They keep people
informed.

What Makes a Good Reporter?

Reporters must tell the truth. They cannot make up facts.

Reporter Skills

✓ good writers   ✓ curious

✓ honest   ✓ good with people

Reporters must be **curious**. They look for important stories. Read all about it!

21

Glossary

curious

excited to learn

news outlets

companies such as TV stations or newspapers that report the news

informed

aware of what is going on

research

to search for answers

interviews

speaks with people to get information

sources

people or places that reporters get information from

To Learn More

AT THE LIBRARY

Anderson, J. L. *Reporter to the Rescue.* Vero Beach, Fla.: Rourke Educational Media, 2019.

Doeden, Matt. *What Is Propaganda?* Minneapolis, Minn.: Lerner Publications, 2020.

Fromowitz, Lori. *12 Great Moments that Changed Newspaper History.* North Mankato, Minn.: 12-Story Library, 2015.

ON THE WEB

Factsurfer.com gives you a safe, fun way to find more information.

1. Go to www.factsurfer.com.

2. Enter "reporters" into the search box and click Q.

3. Select your book cover to see a list of related content.

Index

The images in this book are reproduced through the courtesy of: 2p2play, front cover, pp. 10-11; Anton Gvozdikov, pp. 4-5; Pavel Shlykov, pp. 6-7; fizkes, pp. 8-9; Ana Flasker, pp. 12-13; Holy Polygon, p. 13 (microphone); Carlos E. Santa Maria, p. 13 (camera); Vitaly Zorkin, p. 13 (pencil); eurobanks, p. 13 (notebook); LightField Studios, pp. 14-15; tomazl, pp. 16-17, 20-21; Marmaduke St. John/ Alamy, pp. 18-19; wavebreakmedia, p. 22 (top left); Kaspars Grinvalds, p. 22 (top right); Syda Productions, p. 22 (middle left); Robert Kneschke, p. 22 (middle right); DW labs Incorporated, p. 22 (bottom left); BlueSkyImage, p. 22 (bottom right).